British Library Cataloguing in Publication Data

Prasad, H. Y. Sharada
    Indira Gandhi. — (Famous people)
    1. Gandhi, Indira — Juvenile literature
    2. Prime ministers — India — Biography — Juvenile literature
    I. Title   II. Series
    954.04′092′4   DS481.G23

    ISBN 0-7214-0987-3

INDIRA GANDHI

by H. Y. SHARADA PRASAD
with a foreword by RAJIV GANDHI

FOREWORD

Everyone spends the early years with a very special person - one's mother. My own mother was unusual. She later became Prime Minister of India and famous all over the world, as this book will tell you. Even when I and my younger brother were small, she did a great amount of work for the country. But she spent a good deal of time with us, and took care to make it exciting. She never put on airs of being important or busy. She was full of games and puzzles and stories and bits of poetry. She knew a great deal about history, about books, about art and about trees and birds. She made us feel we were her equal. She refrained from lecturing or giving advice and encouraged us to discuss matters with her. She let us take our own decisions. Later, when I grew up, I regarded her as a friend rather than as someone twenty-six years older.

One of her favourite statements was that a person who was interested became interesting. She remained a great learner - always trying to understand new ideas and re-examine the old.

The world fascinated her. She believed in being mentally and physically alert all the time. That is how she was able to do the work of a dozen people.

I hope this book will help you to understand how Indira Gandhi was spurred from her childhood by the ideal of freedom and a determination to serve the people of India and the whole world.

New Delhi
September 27, 1985

Indira Gandhi was born on 19 November 1917 in Allahabad, one of India's ancient cities, where the Yamuna River flows into the Ganges. She was born in the house of her grandfather, Motilal Nehru.

In Motilal's day, India was part of the British Empire, and Motilal himself lived like a British gentleman, in a large house set in lush, sprawling grounds. He was fond of western clothes and western food. He engaged British governesses for his two daughters and a British tutor for his only son, Jawaharlal.

The old fort of Allahabad, which stands near the place where the Yamuna meets the Ganges (Photo: India International Centre)

Anand Bhawan ("Abode of Joy"), the Nehru family home

Motilal, a strong-willed, high-spirited, generous man known for his laughter and anger, was very fond of his son, and very proud of him. When Jawaharlal was fifteen, Motilal sent him to Harrow, a public school in England. From there he went to Cambridge University. After Cambridge, Jawaharlal studied law, and then returned to India. However, his heart was not in a legal career. Instead, he was deeply interested in politics – and in how to free India from British rule.

Motilal and Jawaharlal Nehru

Mr. & Mrs. Motilal Nehru request the pleasure of your company on the occasion of the marriage of their son Jawaharlal Nehru with Kamala Kaul, daughter of Pandit Jawaharmal Kaul, at Delhi, on the 7th February, 1916, and afterwards on February 8th and 9th, 1916.

Anand Bhawan.
Allahabad   An answer will oblige.

Jawaharlal and Kamala shortly after their wedding

In 1916 Jawaharlal married Kamala Kaul. The wedding took place in Delhi, the capital of India. Motilal and the large party of guests booked a whole train to travel to Delhi. The festivities went on for several days.

Kamala was a shy bride. She was not very familiar with English or western customs and manners. It took time for her to adjust to the ways of Anand Bhawan, or Abode of Joy, as Motilal called his house.

When their daughter was born the following year, Jawaharlal and Kamala called her Indira. They gave her a second name as well — Priyadarshini, or "dear to behold".

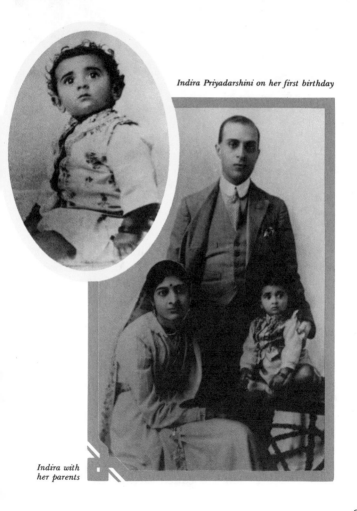

Indira Priyadarshini on her first birthday

Indira with her parents

The Nehru family in 1918.
Indira (centre) is held by her grandmother.

Within two years of Indira's birth the entire way
of life changed at Anand Bhawan. Mahatma Gandhi
had become the leader of India's nationalist
movement, and the Nehrus – especially Indira's
father and grandfather – became his dedicated
followers.

After the First World War Gandhi had hoped that
India would be given a greater degree of self-
government. He was disappointed with what the
British government offered, and began to organise
national protests. He taught that the British should
be opposed non-violently – not with weapons, but by
organising people all over the country to disobey civil
laws, to refuse to pay taxes and to boycott British
goods. Such action was called *satyagraha*.

India in those days imported large quantities of cloth from Britain. Gandhi urged his followers to learn to spin, and to wear cloth made by hand as a sign that the people of India would be self-reliant and not dependent on the goods of other countries. Gandhi and the Indian National Congress (India's leading political party) organised bonfires of British cloth. The Nehrus, known for the stylish clothes they wore, sent their woollens and chiffons to the flames, and everyone at Anand Bhawan began to wear homespun.

Motilal Nehru in homespun

When she was about four, Indira was given a beautiful doll made in England. Though she loved it dearly, she finally decided she must give it up. Years later she described her feelings this way:

For days on end the struggle went on between my love for my doll and what I thought to be my duty towards my country... At last I made my decision and, quivering with tension, I took the doll up on the roof-terrace and set fire to it. Then the tears came as if they would never stop and for some days I was ill. To this day I hate striking a match.

Indira with her mother (first row, centre) and some nationalist workers

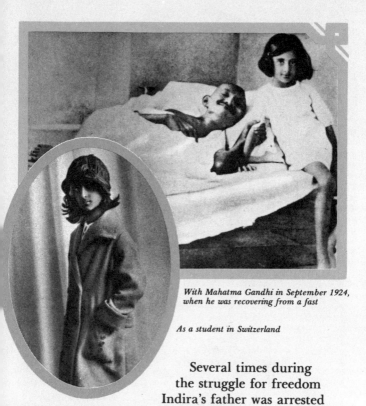

With Mahatma Gandhi in September 1924, when he was recovering from a fast

As a student in Switzerland

Several times during the struggle for freedom Indira's father was arrested and put in prison. In fact, over the next twenty-five years, Jawaharlal spent nearly ten years in jail.

Indira's mother had a baby boy, but he did not live long. Kamala, who had always been somewhat frail, developed a lung disease and in 1926 went to Switzerland for treatment. Indira, who was eight years old at the time, went with her. They stayed in Geneva for some months, where Indira attended the International School. She then attended a school in the nearby town of Bex.

Indira in Switzerland

Indira's father was a great reader and Anand
Bhawan was always full of books. Indira loved
reading from the time she was very young. She read
stories and poems, but what she loved most was
reading about men and women who had fought for
their countries — Joan of Arc of France, Garibaldi of
Italy, Simon Bolivar of South America. She
identified herself with Joan of Arc because she too
was a girl who had stood against British domination.

Jawaharlal often gave Indira challenging books to read. He was also keen that she should be physically fit. Indira had to run and do exercises regularly. She learnt to swim. When the family went to the hills to escape the heat of Allahabad's summer, Indira was so nimble at climbing rocks that her grandfather called her "mountain goat". Mountain trekking remained a passion with Indira throughout her life. She was also fond of skiing.

At home in Allahabad, Indira had her hands full. Mahatma Gandhi was often there, as were other leaders of the Congress. Indira was kept busy running errands for them and shielding them from the public. When there were riots or other disturbances, the injured were brought to Anand Bhawan where Kamala, Indira and others cleaned and bandaged their wounds.

In a pensive moment, at the age of nine

Indira was loved but not spoilt. Because she was gawky and long-nosed, some of her relations called her an ugly duckling. Often left on her own, she learnt to take her own decisions. She was intense and had a searching, questioning mind. But above all she wanted to be worthy of her parents, and to help and protect them. She was proud that their pictures, along with pictures of Mahatma Gandhi, were found in hundreds of thousands of homes.

When Indira was twelve years old, her father became President of the Indian National Congress. At its 1929 session, the Congress had declared that it wanted nothing less than complete independence. Though she was still very young, Indira was one of those who took the pledge of independence which declared:

> *The British Government in India has not only deprived the Indian people of their freedom but has based itself on the exploitation of the masses, and has ruined India economically, politically, culturally and spiritually. We believe, therefore, that India must sever the British connection.*

When told that she had to be eighteen to become a member of the Congress Party, Indira decided to form her own organisation. She gathered together a large number of boys and girls and launched the Vanar Sena or "Monkey Brigade". Its members helped the freedom movement by sewing Congress Party flags, cooking food for people who took part in demonstrations, giving first aid to workers injured in police conflicts and so on.

Indira at about twelve years old, with her parents

Like all fathers, Jawaharlal was fond of giving advice. The advice he gave Indira on her thirteenth birthday was:

> *It is no easy matter to decide what is right and what is not. One little test I shall ask you to apply whenever you are in doubt. Never do anything in secret or anything that you would wish to hide. For the desire to hide anything means that you are afraid, and fear is a bad thing and unworthy of you. Be brave, and all the rest follows.*

Just six weeks later, on the last day of 1930, a mysterious caller telephoned to say that Indira's mother would soon be arrested. Jawaharlal had been in jail for some months, and his wife had been playing an active part in the fight for freedom. On New Year's Eve she and Indira ate dinner together and then read aloud poetry by Tennyson. Early the next morning the police came to take Kamala Nehru away.

Only a few weeks after that Motilal, the old warrior, passed away. Jawaharlal and Kamala had just come out of jail.

A year later Indira's father was back in prison. Over the next eighteen months he wrote letters to Indira relating the stories of the various peoples of the world. He described how some nations had oppressed others and how people struggled for freedom and equality. The letters – 196 in all – were later published under the title *Glimpses of World History*. What Jawaharlal wrote stayed with Indira all her life.

Kamala Nehru

Motilal Nehru in prison, a few years before his death

Indira taking part in a school play

Indira on a trip to Kashmir,
just before entering university

After her grandfather's death Indira was sent to a
school in Poona, a thousand miles away from
Allahabad. It was an unusual school. Its name, the
Pupils' Own School, gave some clue as to how it was
run. The children were expected to think for
themselves and be independent. They visited areas
where poor people lived, and helped the people they
visited. They did not work all the time, however.
Indira learnt to dance and took part in plays at the
Pupils' Own School, too.

After leaving school, Indira went to the Visva-Bharati University, in the east of India. The university had been founded by Rabindranath Tagore, a painter, musician, poet and playwright who had won the Nobel Prize for Literature. Tagore believed that education should produce a "universal" human being, one who was well developed culturally and artistically as well as intellectually. Here Indira came to know people of outstanding talent.

Rabindranath Tagore surrounded by some students at Visva-Bharati. Indira stands second from right

Kamala Nehru, bedridden during her illness

But Indira did not stay long at Visva-Bharati. Her mother's health was failing. Kamala was advised to go to Europe again for treatment, and Indira travelled with her.

It proved to be Kamala's last illness. She died in February 1936. It was some comfort to the family that Jawaharlal had been able to fly to Europe to be with her at the end. She was thirty-six and Indira eighteen. It took Indira a long time to recover from the loss.

In 1938, Indira entered Somerville College, Oxford. Those who studied with her remember her as a quiet but strong-willed person. Once someone asked her why she was studying in Britain when India was fighting the British. She answered, "So as to know the adversary better." She worked for the India League, which put forward India's case for freedom in Britain.

Indian freedom was not the only cause that kept Indira busy. She collected funds for China, which had been attacked by Japan, and attended meetings to protest against the Nazis.

Indira in Europe

One of the reasons Indira decided to study in England was that Feroze Gandhi was there. Feroze, five years older than Indira, was also from Allahabad. Politics excited him and he had helped Kamala Nehru in her work. He had proposed to Indira when she was only sixteen but she had turned him down. Feroze did not give up. He and Indira met again in Europe, and his persistence paid off.

Feroze Gandhi in London

Indira and Feroze on their way back to India from England, 1941

Portrait of Indira in London, taken by Feroze

But Indira fell seriously ill. She was advised to go to Switzerland for rest. Within a few days of her arrival there, the Second World War broke out. Britain was cut off. It was many months before Indira could return to England, and then only after a long wait in Portugal. She filled her time by teaching English to refugees.

She and Feroze left England and sailed for India in 1941. On the way, their ship docked in South Africa, where Indira was angered by the laws imposing bans against black people. She made a fiery speech against racialism.

Indira and Feroze at their wedding

Indira and Feroze were married on 26 March 1942 at Anand Bhawan. They observed the old Hindu wedding ritual of going round the sacred fire seven times, although Feroze was not a Hindu. He was a Parsi, a follower of the ancient religion of Zoroastrianism. And though his surname was Gandhi, he was no relation to Mahatma Gandhi.

Among the wedding gifts were two that Indira prized in particular – a piece of cloth woven by Mahatma Gandhi and a sari made from yarn that had been spun by her father.

There was great political tension in India at the time. The war was not going too well for Britain and the Allies. Japan had overrun country after country and was moving close to India. The Indian National Congress demanded the right to defend itself. The British turned down the demand. Self-government only after victory, they said. Freedom now, insisted Mahatma Gandhi. He planned a new *satyagraha* to make the British quit India. But the British arrested Mahatma Gandhi, Jawaharlal Nehru and all the top leaders of the Congress as well as thousands of other people all over the country.

Feroze and Indira, who were in Bombay, went back to Allahabad to organise resistance. It was announced that Indira would address a rally there. Policemen and soldiers were all around as the crowd gathered. Feroze watched from a nearby building. When Indira began her speech he saw her surrounded by police, with a bayonet almost touching her. He rushed out at the policemen. Both Feroze and Indira were taken to the Allahabad jail. There they spent the next few months, but apart from each other — she in the women's section of the prison and he in the men's wing.

Indira was not allowed to receive letters or have visitors. She therefore had no link with her father. But she was determined not to be defeated. Eight months later she came out of jail. "It was like coming suddenly out of a dark passage. I was dazzled with the rush of life, the many hues and textures, the scale of sounds and the range of ideas," she said.

Six months later Feroze was released, and they set up house together once again. On 20 August 1944 their first son, Rajiv, was born. Jawaharlal, who was still in jail, wrote very solicitous letters, giving Indira advice and suggesting names for his grandson. Indira said the birth of Rajiv was the happiest moment in her life. Of motherhood she said: "To bring a new being into this world, to see its tiny perfection, and to dream of its future greatness is the most moving of all experiences."

Jawaharlal Nehru and the leaders of the Congress were freed in the middle of 1945. Mahatma Gandhi had been released earlier. The war was about to end. The British knew they could not hold India much longer. They opened negotiations with the leaders of the Congress. At the same time the Muslim League, another of India's political parties, demanded that a separate state of Pakistan should be created, made up of those areas of India where Muslims were in the majority. Until the issue was resolved an interim government of Indian leaders was formed, with Jawaharlal Nehru as its head.

Jawaharlal wanted Indira to look after his household. Indira took to dividing her time between her father in Delhi and her husband in Lucknow. Her second son, Sanjay, was born in December 1946.

Photograph opposite:
Indira with Rajiv

The attempts to prevent the splitting of India failed. India and Pakistan came into being as separate dominions – India at midnight of 14 August 1947 and Pakistan a few hours earlier. Lord Mountbatten, the last Viceroy of India, read the British monarch's proclamation of India's freedom. And, in a speech that became famous, Jawaharlal Nehru declared: "Long years ago we made a tryst with destiny, and now the time comes when we shall redeem our pledge... At the stroke of the midnight hour, when the world sleeps, India will awake to life and freedom." Jawaharlal Nehru became the first Prime Minister of free India.

*A crowd at Vijay Chowk, New Delhi,
celebrates India's freedom,
15 August 1947*

Because the country was partitioned, millions of
people moved from Pakistan to India and from India
to Pakistan. They were filled with fear and hate, and
hundreds of thousands were killed. At Mahatma
Gandhi's request, Indira went to work in the riot-
torn areas of Delhi, helping people in need and
attempting to calm the troubled atmosphere. She
worked hard and tirelessly, and Mahatma Gandhi
praised her dedication. But that man of peace was
himself killed by a fanatic just a few months later.

Teen Murti House, Delhi, Jawaharlal Nehru's home during his years as Prime Minister

Indira was finally persuaded to stay in Delhi and be her father's hostess. For years she had acted as his secretary, typed letters for him and travelled with him. She had read the proofs of the book he wrote in his final term of imprisonment, *The Discovery of India*. Now there were international statesmen to meet and foreign countries to visit. She also had her little sons to take care of. She set aside as much time as she could to be with them. A mother's company, she said, was like water and air to a child.

With Rajiv and Sanjay on the lawn of Teen Murti House

In the gardens at Anand Bhawan,
shortly after being made
Congress Party President
(Photo: T. S. Satyan)

Indira with her father at a Congress Party meeting
(Photo: Indian Express)

But politics did not leave her alone. Indira was inducted into the main committees of the Congress Party, and in 1959 she was elected its President.

In September 1960 Feroze died of a heart attack. Within four years Jawaharlal Nehru was also dead. He had been Prime Minister of India for seventeen years. Indira Gandhi hoped that she could now retire to the high mountains. But the new Prime Minister, Lal Bahadur Shastri, would not hear of it. He insisted that she join his cabinet. She was given charge of the Ministry of Information and Broadcasting.

With her father at Dehra Dun on 26 May 1964, the day before his death

Shastri's stay in office was short. Early in January 1966 he died unexpectedly. Once again the country had to find a new Prime Minister. The leaders of the Congress thought that Indira would be the best choice. The other contender for the post was Morarji Desai. Indira easily won the election, and she was sworn in as Prime Minister on 24 January 1966. She was to remain in that office for eleven years.

Indira being sworn in as Prime Minister

In the 1967 general election Indira's party, the Congress, was returned to power but with a reduced majority. Some of the policies adopted by Indira Gandhi were opposed by her colleagues, and there was a split within the party. Indira Gandhi's wing won a huge victory in the 1971 elections.

But one of the candidates who had opposed her went to court saying that she had won the election unfairly. The case went on for four years. In June 1975 her election was set aside but the court ruled that she might continue to be Prime Minister. Still, several political parties demanded her resignation. Some of them asked the police and the army to revolt as, in their view, Indira Gandhi had lost the moral right to be Prime Minister. She placed the country under a state of emergency, arresting a large number of opposition leaders and workers, and introduced censorship of the press.

Twenty-one months later, in March 1977, Indira Gandhi called for an election. Her faith was in the people's right to decide. But much that had happened during the emergency was not to the liking of the people. Her party was soundly defeated. The opposition leaders who had been jailed by her won by large margins. Various opposition parties merged to form a single party, the Janata Party. The new government appointed a commission to inquire into Indira Gandhi's actions. Her younger son, Sanjay, who had become prominent in national politics during the emergency, was arrested.

Some meetings that took place during Indira's second term as Prime Minister:

With Pope John Paul II at the Vatican, November 1981

It was not long before the tide of people's sympathy began flowing back towards Indira Gandhi. She won a by-election to the House of the People, one of the houses of Parliament. However, the House expelled her and she had to spend some days in jail.

The groups which had formed the Janata Party broke up. The new government was compelled to call a general election halfway through its five-year term. In the January 1980 polls for the House of the People, Indira Gandhi was swept back to power.

Within six months, tragedy struck her. Sanjay was killed while flying an aircraft. Indira bore the blow with great calm.

With Queen Elizabeth at the President's House, New Delhi, November 1983

With President Ronald Reagan at the White House, July 1982

Despite her popularity, Indira Gandhi, like all political leaders, had her share of enemies. On the morning of 31 October 1984, as Indira came out onto the lawns of her house for a television interview, her enemies shot her dead. She was nineteen days short of her sixty-seventh birthday.

Indira Gandhi died as she would have wanted to, active until the last minute. For years she had worked sixteen hours a day, rarely taking holidays. Her energy, even when she was in her sixties, amazed people. She was fond of saying that there was a vast store of power within everyone but people failed to recognise and develop it.

Her grandchildren found her fun to be with. She had a wide range of interests: painting, folk music, dance, poetry, flowers and birds, the conservation of nature. She believed that life could not be broken up into compartments, and that in order to achieve inner poise, one must know the unity of all living things.

Her guiding principle was to do her duty, unmindful of whether the fruit was bitter or sweet. Only the evening before her death she had spoken to a large gathering a thousand miles away from Delhi, and said:

> *I am here today, but I may not be here tomorrow. Nobody knows how many attempts have been made to shoot me. I do not care whether I live or die. I have enjoyed a long life and I am proud that I spent the whole of it in the service of my people. I shall continue to serve until my last breath. And when I die, I can say that every drop of my blood will invigorate India and strengthen it.*

Indira in March 1984, some months before her death

A family portrait, 1974. Left to right: Sanjay; Rajiv; Indira; Rajiv's son and daughter; Maneka Gandhi (Sanjay's wife); Sonia Gandhi (Rajiv's wife)

A few scenes from the public life of Indira Gandhi:

1 *Signing a copy of her father's autobiography, 1937*

2 *In Washington DC, with her father and President and Mrs John F. Kennedy, 1961*

3 *With Prime Minister Margaret Thatcher at a conference at Cancun, Mexico, October 1981*

4 *With Rajiv as he dons a spacesuit at Star City, Soviet Union, September 1982*

5 *Receiving the Order of the Golden Ark, for her work in nature conservation, from Prince Bernhard of the Netherlands, May 1982*

3

4

5